WINNING JERSEY

TIME
4 hours

MATERIALS
Cotton baseball jersey
Size 10° seed beads
Size D beading thread

NOTIONS
Number stencils
Quilter's pencil or light-colored pen
Size 12° beading or sharps needle
Embroidery hoop
Scissors

Bead this fun jersey for a birthday or any day that has numerical significance. The one shown here celebrates adulthood for a special 21-year-old.

Step 1: Lay out the jersey absolutely flat. Place the stencils down so that they are straight. Use the quilter's pencil or light pen to stencil the numbers on the chest. Remove the stencils.

Step 2: Place the embroidery hoop around the numbers.

Step 3: Back stitch the stencil: Using about a yard of thread, knot the end and *pass through the fabric wrong side to right side at the corner of one of the stencil marks. String 3 beads. Lay the beads down against the fabric and pass through the fabric from right side to wrong wide right in front of the last bead strung. Come back up through the fabric where the second bead lies. Pass through the second and third bead strung.

Step 4: Rep Step 3 from *, following the shape of the stencils.

SPIRALING EYEGLASS CHAIN

TIME

8 hours

MATERIALS

Size 11° seed beads in two colors ("inside" beads and "outside" beads)
Size D beading thread in color to complement beads
2 eyeglass chain findings

NOTIONS

Size 12° beading or sharps needle
Scissors

Afriend once told me, "This is the best gift I ever received." Though simple, the chain is a time-eater, so choose your colors carefully to accent the spiral effect—you'll be looking at those colors for a while!

Step 1: Using a yard of thread and leaving a 6" tail, string 8 inside beads. Pass back through the seventh and eighth beads just strung to create a circle. Tie a square knot and pass through all the beads just strung again, exiting at the eighth bead.

Step 2: String 4 inside beads and 3 outside beads. Pass through the inside beads (Figure 1).

Step 3: String 1 inside and 3 outside beads. Pass through 3 inside beads and pass back through the last inside bead strung (Figure 2). Let these outside beads rest next to previous row's outside beads.

Repeat Step 2 (Figure 3) until your chain is 24" then repeat Step 1. Finish by trimming all tails and adding the eyeglass holder findings.

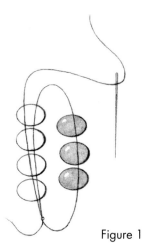

Figure 1

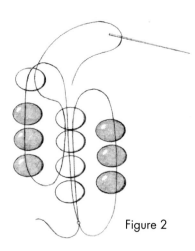

Figure 2

Figure 3

GREAT BANGLE BRACELET

TIME
15 minutes

MATERIALS
SoftFlex® beading wire
Assorted beads
Crimp beads
Clasp (Magna Loc clasp used for this example)

NOTIONS
Measuring tape
Wire cutters
Crimping pliers

This bracelet gives you the basics for bead stringing. If you make one for a friend, be prepared for a big hug!

Step 1: Measure your wrist or your friend's and add 2". Use that measurement to cut the wire. String 2 crimp beads and one side of the clasp. Pass back through the 2 crimp beads and crimp.

Step 2: String the assorted beads in a way that you desire—just be sure that the first few beads cover the beading wire tail.

Step 3: Check the desired length again and adjust the beads as necessary. Finish by stringing 2 crimp beads and the other side of the clasp. Pass back through the crimp beads. Pull tight and squeeze the crimp beads. Tuck the tail into as many beads as possible and trim the end.

BEAUTIFUL BEADED BUTTONS

This is a special gift for anyone who knows how to sew on a button, but if your friend knits or makes garments, a set of buttons will be a special treat.

TIME

½ hour per button

MATERIALS

Size 11° seed beads
Size D beading thread
¼ yard satin to match beads
⅝" button-covering and metal buttons

NOTIONS

Size 12° beading or sharps needle
Dressmaker's pencil
Scissor

Step 1: Use the manufacturer's directions to cover the button face with the satin.

Step 2: Thread your needle using ½ yard of thread. Knot the end. Make a hidden stitch at the base of the button. Sew your needle to the button's face.

Step 3: Back stitch [see below] on the face of the button with beads. Make a simple circle around the rim of the button or completely cover the face starting from the center and working your way to the edge.

Step 4: When you're finished beading, pass your needle under the fabric so it exits at the edge of the button. Pass your needle under the fabric again and pass down the side of the button. Tie a knot and trim thread close to work.

Back stitch

Also known as "return stitch" and "running stitch." Begin by passing the needle through the fabric, from wrong side to right side, at the place where the first bead is to go. String a bead and pass the needle back through the fabric to the left of the bead. Bring the needle back through the fabric to the right of the bead, pass back through the bead, and back down through the fabric. Continue with one backstitch per bead. You can sew up to three beads per stitch by stringing three beads and backstitching only through the third as shown below.

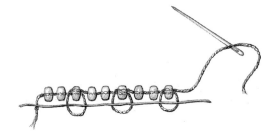

STONE DONUT NECKLACE

TIME

15 minutes

MATERIALS

Stone donut
Assorted wide-holed beads
4' round black leather cord

NOTIONS

Scissors

This project is about as easy as beading gets! The resulting necklace is so elegant, your friend will think you bought it from an expensive boutique.

NECKLACE

Step 1: Measure and cut 1 yard of cord. Fold it in half and make a lark's head knot through the middle of the donut (see Figure 1).

Step 2: Place the donut in the middle of your chest and pull each cord end up and around your neck so that each end sits on the opposite side from which it started. Make a mental note * as to where this spot is. Take the necklace off.

Step 3: Put one cord end where it was at * in Step 2. Using about 3" of cord, begin wrapping the cord back on itself. When through, weave the remaining cord through the coil and pull tight (Figure 2).

DANGLES

Step 4: Measure and cut two 6" pieces of cord. Hold them together and make a lark's head knot through the other side of the donut, opposite the necklace.

Step 5: String the assorted wide-holed beads to your liking on each of the four cords. Finish each cord with a half knot (Figure 3).

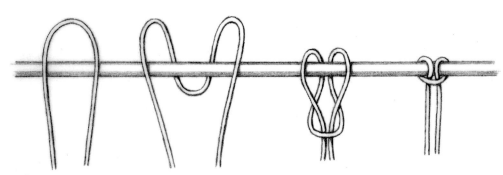

Figure 1

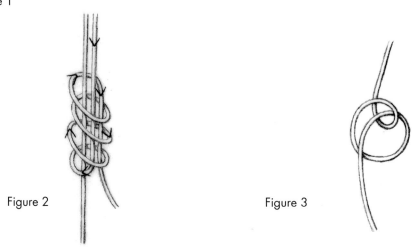

Figure 2

Figure 3

CREATIVE CARD CASE

This is a perfect gift for a person starting their first job, or anyone for whom a regular old card case just won't do.

BEADWORK

Step 1: Create a flat peyote-stitched rectangle of beadwork that measures the same as a business or calling card (the rectangle shown here is 30 beads wide by 35 beads long). See Figure 1 for peyote stitch instruction. Follow the chart shown here or create your own design.

CASE

Step 2: Measure and mark the leather widthwise to match the business card and add ½". Measure and mark the leather lengthwise to match the card and add 2". Cut the leather. Fold (rough sides together) one end under 1" and glue. At the other end, use a scissors to gently curve the corners.

Step 3: Fold the leather together (rough sides together) and place the card so it fits comfortably inside. Arrange the fold so that one end sticks out 1" from the glued end and looks like a flap. Tape the leather together where the flap and the glued end meet.

Step 4: Using a ruler and a ballpoint pen, mark the leather at ⅜" intervals all around. Using a leatherworking punch or a drill with a small point, make small holes where you made marks.

Step 5: Using a yard of metallic thread and the holes you punched in Step 4, whip stitch (see page 19) the case edges together. When you reach the flap-side holes, just sew your thread through the holes as decoration. As an added decorative touch, whip stitch in the other direction to create a series of Xs.

FINISHING

Step 6: Using a yard of red beading thread, stitch the peyote-stitched rectangle to the metallic whip stitching on the leather case. Don't worry about passing through the beads. Instead, make the connection at the thread between the beads and the metallic thread.

Step 7: Measure the halfway point on the flap and stick a Velcro button here. Carefully unpeel the other side of the button and fold it over to the case side.

TIME

10 hours

MATERIALS

Size 11° red, green, yellow, and metallic rainbow seed beads
Size D black or red beading thread
10" × 3" piece of red leather
E-600 glue
Tape
Size E metallic thread
Size D red beading thread
Velcro button

NOTIONS

Size 12° beading or sharps needle
Scissors
Business card
Ruler
Ballpoint pen
Leatherworking punch or drill with small bit
Sewing needle

Even-count flat peyote

Begin by stringing an even number of beads, twice the number you want in one row. These beads will become the first and second rows. Create the next row by stringing one bead and passing through the second-to-last bead of the previous row. String another bead and pass through the fourth-to-last bead of the previous row. Continue adding one bead at a time, passing over every other bead of the previous row.

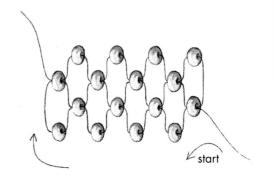

start

BOX-O-SNOW

Whether or not you live in a snowy place, you can make a box of snow for friends who don't. Your winter wonderland wishes are certain to bring cheer.

TIME

15 minutes per snowflake

MATERIALS

Size 11° seed beads in shades of white and silver
Assorted bugle beads in shades of white and silver
White D beading thread

NOTIONS

Size 12° beading or sharps needle
Scissors

BASIC SNOWFLAKE

Round 1: Using about 2' of thread and leaving a 3" tail, string 6 beads. Tie into a foundation circle and pass through the first bead just added.

Round 2: String 1 bead and pass through the next bead on the foundation circle. Continue around, adding a bead and passing through a bead until you have added 6 beads in all. Exit from the first bead you added in this round.

Round 3: String 3 beads. Pass through the second bead you added in Round 2 to make a picot. Continue around, adding 3 beads and passing through a bead until you have added 18 beads in all (Figure 1).

Weave your thread through all the beads again and trim the working and tail threads close to the work.

Once you have the basic snowflake under your hat, branch out! Use bugle and seed bead combinations at or between the picots to make variations.

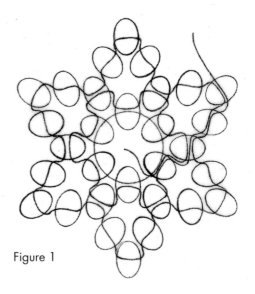

Figure 1

QUICK AND FUN BEADED FRAME

This is a quickie frame for any-time, anywhere. Your friend can glue a magnet on the back, put it on an easel, or put it in or *on* her scrapbook! Maybe she'll put your picture in it.

TIME
1 hour

MATERIALS
Photograph
White or black card stock paper slightly larger than photograph
Glue stick
Size 11° seed beads
Size D beading thread in color to complement the beads

NOTIONS
Ruler
Sharp pencil
Large needle
Size 12° beading or sharps needle
Scissors

Step 1: Cut your cardstock ¼" larger than your photograph.

Step 2: Center the photograph on the cardstock. Use the glue stick to adhere the photograph to the cardstock. Allow to dry.

Step 3: Just next to the photograph, use the pencil to mark the cardstock at ⅛" intervals.

Step 4: Use the large needle to punch holes in the marks made in Step 3.

Step 5: Use double knotted thread to pass through from back to front one of the holes punched in Step 4.

Step 6: String 5 beads and pass through from back to front into the next hole on the card (Figure 1).

Repeat Step 6 all around the card. Tie a knot after the last stitch.

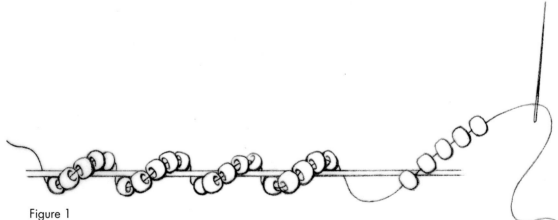

Figure 1

ELEGANT BRIDAL DOILY

Your friend who is about to become a bride will happily put this embellished doily in her trousseau! She can use it at the registry table to set her pen on, as an accent for her ring bearer pillow, or as an embellishment for her photo book. Use the bride's wedding colors to make the doily extra special.

TIME

3–4 hours

MATERIALS

Pre-made rectangular lace doily
Size 11° white seed beads
2mm white (or other) sequins
4mm white (or other) sequins
Dangle beads
Size D white beading thread

NOTIONS

Size 12° beading or sharps needle
Scissors

Step 1: Choose a spot near the center of the doily on the ribbon edging. Using a yard of thread, tie a knot and pass the needle through the fabric from wrong side to right side. *String 1 4mm sequin and a white bead. Pass through from the right side to the wrong side, near to where you originally exited. Repeat from * around the square.

Step 2: Fill the corner edging with sequins as you did in Step 1. Add a dangle bead at each corner by stringing the dangle and 3 seed beads. Pass back through the dangle and pull tight.

Step 3: Fill the side edging with sequins as you did in Step 1, but use the 2mm sequins.

OLD FASHIONED BUTTON NECKLACE

I recently saw a necklace like this in a ladies' fashion magazine for $300, but I also remember seeing one in my granny's jewelry box! In any case, the pearlescent snaky look makes this necklace go with anything, and the receiver of this gift will certainly be pleased.

TIME

1 hour

MATERIALS

Approximately 260½" white
two-hole buttons
Size D white beading thread

NOTIONS

Sewing needle
Scissors

Step 1: Measure and cut 6' of thread. Thread a needle, double the thread, and knot the ends together.

Step 2: String one button passing through one hole, wrong side to right side. Pass through the other hole, right side to wrong side. (If your buttons have four holes, use only two of them.) Pass through the loop created by the knot in the thread to secure your thread to the button (Figure 1).

Step 3: String one button by passing through one hole, wrong side to right side. Pass through the other hole, right side to wrong side. Hold this button and the button previously strung wrong side to wrong side.

Step 4: Rep Step 3 until you reach your desired length (Figure 1).

Step 5: When you reach the end, attach the first and last buttons, wrong side to wrong side. Finish off by tying knots between buttons near the wrong sides.

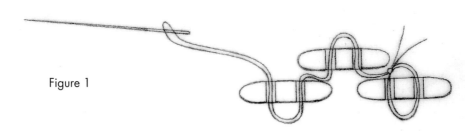

Figure 1

COASTERS FIT FOR KINGS AND QUEENS

I love these coasters because they remind me of what a king or queen would set their rum punch on. I also like the idea of making up four of these, wrapping them in gold ribbon, and adding four glass mugs as a gift. Maybe you'll get invited back for tea and crumpets!

TIME

1½ hours per coaster

MATERIALS

2 pieces of 5" × 5" red velvet
Red sewing thread
Size 10 gold seed beads
Size 8 gold seed beads
Size D gold beading thread

NOTIONS

Ruler
Sewing machine
Scissors
Pen
Size 12° beading needle
Iron

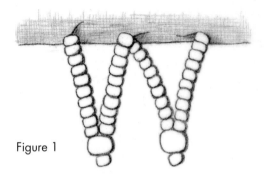

Figure 1

COASTER

Step 1: Place the two pieces of velvet face to face. Leaving a 2" opening at one edge, use the sewing machine and red thread to sew all edges with a ⅜" seam.

Step 2: Use the 2" opening to turn the coaster inside-out. Put a pen inside to poke out the corners.

Step 3: Use the red sewing thread to sew the opening. Iron.

EMBELLISHMENT

Step 4: Knot the end in one yard of gold beading thread. *Pass through the fabric at the very edge of the coaster from the back side to the front side. String 10 size 10°s, 1 size 8°, and 1 size 10°. Pass back through the size 8°. String 10 size 10°s. Sew into the fabric ½" from your first stitch from the back side to the front side (Figure 1).

Step 5: Repeat Step 4 from * all around the coaster. To finish, simply sew several stitches at the edge of the coaster, make a knot, and trim close to the work.

PIRATE'S COVE EARRINGS

TIME

½ hour

MATERIALS

Six 3mm silver beads
Six ¼" Bali silver daisies
Two 6mm leopard jasper beads
Two 18mm cranberry teardrop beads
Two silver headpins

NOTIONS

Wire cutters
Round-nose pliers
Flat-nose pliers

These elegant earrings look like something from a pirate's cache, but they take only minutes to make, and they'll delight any recipient.

Step 1: String 1 silver bead, 1 Bali daisy, 1 teardrop, 1 Bali daisy, 1 jasper, 1 Bali daisy, and 1 silver bead on the head pin.

Step 2: Grasp the head-pin wire from the top of the last bead and bend the wire over to make a ninety-degree angle .

Step 3: Grasp the head-pin wire firmly with the round-nose pliers, right at the bend you created in Step 2. Grasp the tip of the head-pin wire with the flat-nose pliers and swing the wire down, around, and past the round-nose pliers to make a loop.

Step 4: Straighten the loop by shifting the round-nose and bending the wire to the proper position.

Step 5: Position the round-nose in the loop and hold the wire end with the flat-nose. Hold the round-nose tightly as you use the flat-nose to wrap the stem of the wire all the way down to the last bead strung.

Step 6: Finish by cutting the wire close to the wrap. Push the wire end in line with the wrap by gently squeezing it with the flat-nose pliers.

MEDIEVAL KNITTED WIRE NECKLACE

The beauty of this knitted wire necklace is the chain-mail look it gives to the final piece. It's the perfect gift for the friend who likes big, bold jewelry.

Step 1: Without cutting the wire from the spool, thread the wire down the hole of the dolly so that it clears about 5". Bend up the side so you can hold onto the wire while you work.

Step 2: Wrap the working wire around the pegs of the dolly counterclockwise, wrapping from inside to outside of the pegs (Figure 1). Go around all four pegs a second time. *Use the crochet hook to lift the lower loop over the upper loop and up and over the top of the peg. Rep from * for all four pegs.

Step 3: Continue your loose chain until it reaches about 1'.

Step 4: Finish chain by cutting the wire from the spool and leaving a 5" tail. Thread the wire end through each loop on the pegs. Remove the loops from the pegs and pull on the wire end to tighten. PT all four loops again and bend the wire to create a knot.

Step 5: Pull the loose chain through progressively smaller holes on the draw plate until the chain won't get any smaller. Use the extra wire to create a loop at each end of the chain.

Step 6: Attach an S clasp at each end of the wire to each loop.

Step 7: Make a double loop at one end of 7" of the 20-gauge wire. String one 7mm bead, 1 tear drop, one 7mm, one 10mm, 1 Bali silver bead, one 10mm, 1 Bali silver bead, one 10mm, 1 Bali silver bead, one 10mm, one 7mm, 1 tear drop, and one 7mm. Make a double loop at the other end of the wire.

Step 8: Attach a split ring to each double loop created in Step 7. Attach the split rings to the S clasps.

TIME

3 hours

MATERIALS

26-gauge silver wire
20-gauge silver wire
Four 7mm iridescent glass beads
Two 18mm cranberry teardrops
Four 10mm cranberry glass beads
Three 16mm Bali silver beads
2 silver S clasps
2 large silver split rings

NOTIONS

Knitting dolly or spool with four staples or finishing nails
Size 5 to 10 steel crochet hook or stylus
Metal or wooden draw plate
Wire cutters
Round-nose pliers

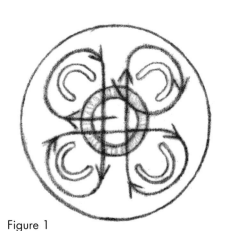

Figure 1

Knitting Dolly

SLICK CANDLESTICK

Terrifically Tacky Tape® and strung beads mean that making this gift is a breeze. You'll get by with giving just one of these fabulous candlesticks if you keep the colors bold and the designs fun. Using large size 8° beads makes the job quick, but you can also experiment with smaller beads to achieve more detail.

TIME
1–2 hours

MATERIALS
Candlestick
Terrifically Tacky Tape®
Size 8° seed beads
Size D beading thread

NOTIONS
Size 10° beading or sewing needle
Scissors

Step 1: Apply the tape to the first inch on the candlestick. Do not remove the tape's protective coating.

Step 2: String your beads. Begin with a tension bead and then a pattern of beads.

Step 3: Remove the protective coating from the tape and lay your beads onto the tape. Press your beads into the tape.

Step 4: Repeat Steps 1, 2, and 3, laying down tape, stringing beads, and pressing the strung beads into the tape until you completely cover the surface of the candlestick.

OCEAN GODDESS POCKET SHRINE

This is a gift I made for myself! Since I live in a dry climate, I keep this "pocket shrine" in my purse at all times so I can remember how important liquidity is in my life. I used an ocean goddess for my pocket shrine, but you might choose any icon, such as a crucifix, Buddha, hand, or labyrinth.

TIME
2 hours

MATERIALS
Small rectangular candy tin (I used Altoids)
Collage materials (photographs, magazine clips, handmade paper, etc.)
Glue
One 1" × 2" piece of cardstock
One 1½" × 5" length of ribbon
Sewing thread
Size B beading thread
Size 11° seed beads
Assortment of beads (pearls, bugles, etc.)
One ¾" icon (crucifix, Buddha, hand, etc.)
One 1" magnet
Hot glue stick

NOTIONS
Scissors
Sewing machine
Size 12° beading or sharps needle
Hot glue gun

Step 1: Use the glue to cover the candy tin with images and papers that please you. Cover the entire inside and outside. Allow to dry.

Step 2: Fold the ribbon over the cardstock and use the sewing machine to sew it in place.

Step 3: Using a yard of thread, knot the end and come through the cardstock and ribbon from wrong side to right side about ⅛" from the edge. Make kinky fringe all around the ribbon using seed and other beads.

KINKY FRINGE

String 10 beads. This is your base string. Skip the last bead strung and pass back through three more. String 4 beads. Skip the last bead strung and pass back through the three others just strung. Continue up the base string so that you have a branched string of beadwork.

Step 4: Hot glue the icon to the center of the ribbon on the right side. Hot glue the magnet to the center of the ribbon on the wrong side. Place the magnet in the tin.

Figure 1

BEADS AND MIRRORS FRAME

TIME
10 hours

MATERIALS
Size 10° seed beads in silver, orange, magenta, light blue, and green
Four ½" × ½" beveled mirrors
Size D beading thread
14-count black Aida cloth
Glue
3½" × 4½" black frame

NOTIONS
White quilter's pencil
Embroidery hoop
Size 10° beading or sewing needle
Scissors

This frame is an eye catcher for any room or any friend. The bold colors and uneven beadwork created by the large 10° beads give the piece an exotic, imported look. Bead the design shown here or experiment using your own designs. Add interest by gluing on larger beads or small mirrors within the design.

Step 1: Pull the Aida cloth tightly across the embroidery hoop. Center and transfer the pattern below to the Aida cloth using the quilter's pencil.

Step 2: Glue the mirrors to the Aida cloth.

Step 3: Use backstitch (Figure 1) to follow the pattern.

Step 4: After you finish backstitching, remove the beadwork from the hoop and follow Figure 1 for trim instructions.

Step 5: Fold the cloth flaps underneath the beadwork and glue. Allow to dry.

Step 6: Glue the beadwork to the frame.

Trim

Figure 1

VOTIVE HOLDERS

TIME
1–2 hours

MATERIALS
Square glass votive candleholder
Large (½"–1") glass or plastic beads
Quick drying two-part clear epoxy
India ink
Papier-maché (or paper clay)
Votive candle or tea light

NOTIONS
Paper towels
Flat wooden stick
Latex gloves

These quick and easy votive candleholders bring warmth and cheer inside or outside the house.

Step 1: Mix the two-part epoxy according to manufacturer's directions.

Step 2: Lay down a paper towel and put the candleholder on its side on top of the paper towel. Use the wooden stick to spread a thin layer of the epoxy on the side of the candleholder that's facing up.

Step 3: Very carefully lay the beads on this side and allow the epoxy to dry.

Step 4: Repeat Steps 2 and 3 to cover all four sides.

Step 5: Put on the latex gloves. Mix the papier-maché according to manufacturer's directions. Mix in enough India ink to make the papier-maché black.

Step 6: Press the papier-maché into the spaces left between the beads on the candleholder. Carefully wipe away any excess so that you get the effect of a stained glass window.

CLEO'S MEMORY WIRE BRACELET

TIME
15 minutes

MATERIALS
Assorted beads
Memory wire

NOTIONS
Round-nose pliers

Making a memory-wire bracelet is about as close to instant gratification as beadwork gets. Memory wire is a product that retains its Slinky-like shape even when it's stretched or twisted.

The stuff is so tough that you shouldn't use your jewelry snips to cut it because you'll damage them. Instead, bend the wire back and forth several times until it breaks.

Step 1: Use a round-nose pliers to coil one end of the wire to act as a stopper.

Step 2: String beads as desired.

Step 3: Rep Step 1, ensuring the beads are snug.